C000284244

How to
Treble
Your Sales
Results in
Six Weeks!

The ultimate sales resource guide
packed with proven, practical &
easy to implement sales strategies

Fiona Challis

*Inspirational speaker, business growth
& sales conversion expert*

How to
Treble
Your Sales Results in Six Weeks!

The ultimate sales resource guide
packed with proven, practical &
easy to implement sales strategies

Fiona Challis

How to Treble Your Sales Results in Six Weeks!

The ultimate sales resource guide packed with
proven, practical & easy to implement sales strategies

Copyright © 2010 Fiona Challis. All rights reserved.
First paperback edition printed 2010 in the United Kingdom

A catalogue record for this book is available from the British
Library.

ISBN 978-1-907308-06-2

No part of this book shall be reproduced or transmitted in any
form or by any means, electronic or mechanical, including photo-
copying, recording, or by any information retrieval system without written permission of the publisher.

Designed and Set by The Book Refinery Ltd

Printed by the MPG Books Group in the UK

Although every precaution has been taken in the preparation of
this book, the publisher and author assume no responsibility for
errors or omissions. Neither is any liability assumed for damages
resulting from the use of this information contained herein.

Contents

Introduction

This book will do more to increase your sales results than any other publication or article you have read. It is based on more than 15 years of experience in direct and indirect sales, telephone selling and face to face selling in both the Business to Business [B2B] and Business to Consumer [B2C] marketplaces and is packed with sales techniques and strategies that are all easy to implement.

Everything you learn in this book has been tried and tested in the field. The sales techniques I introduce have already enabled thousands of sales people, internationally, to achieve levels of success that they never dreamed possible. In fact some of them gained up to 400% increase in sales results!!

It has taken a long time for me to actually sit down and write this book however, after much convincing from my customers and colleagues, I decided to take time out of running training courses to complete the book and help as many sales people and business owners as possible to achieve a higher level of sales success.

After reading this book you will be able to dismiss the myth of sales being tough and to understand that sales is simply a process of asking the right questions, to the right prospects at the right time and then presenting them with the right solution.

You will be better equipped to sell on value instead of price and you will create a structured sales process that will help you to gain more new business prospects and increased spend from your existing prospects. You will have a better understanding of why a 'will factor' is crucial to your success in sales and how having the right plan and taking the right actions can treble your sales results in just six weeks!

You will improve your attitude, your sales techniques and increase your bottom line!

So without further ado, enjoy the book and remember, your mind is like a parachute; it works best when it is open!

Enjoy

Fiona

Acknowledgements

I would like to dedicate this book to my beautiful son Jamie, who makes everything worthwhile and to my friends and family, for their love and dedicated support.

I wish to thank all of our loyal customers for taking action, implementing our training and achieving levels of sales success that have enabled us to become a leading provider in the world of sales training and development. It has been a privilege to work with you!

A special thank you to Jonathan Jay, Founder and Managing Director of NABO (National Association of Business Owners) for giving me the inspiration [and the kick up the assets] that I needed to actually sit down and write this book and a special thanks to Alexa Whitten from The Book Refinery, for helping it to see the light of day. Ed Rivis, the guru of successful web marketing, for his words of wisdom and Paul Green from Publicity Heaven for his help and support in promoting my book. You have all made what appeared as impossible, into something that is possible and actually very fulfilling and enjoyable!!

Chapter 1: A Little Thing That Makes a Big Difference

Over the years I have worked with thousands of sales people all over the globe and every time I ask **'who would like to more than treble their sales results?'**, every single hand shoots up the air as fast as they can, as ultimately achieving increased sales would make their life so much easier. They would be able to earn a lot more money and have all of the luxuries they want in life.

However, from my years of experience of being in sales and leading and developing sales people, I also know that if I follow that question with, **'Who believes they can more than treble their sales results in just six weeks?'**, only a portion of hands will go up.

The people who raise their hands and believe that they can achieve all have one thing in common. It is a little thing that makes a very big difference in sales and these people have it in abundance. It is ATTITUDE.

Believe And You Will Achieve

These people believe they can achieve increased sales results. They have chosen to have the attitude of a top performer and they will be willing to do what it takes to achieve.

So before we go any further, let me ask you, do you believe you can treble your sales results in just six weeks?

Congratulations if you do believe that you can do it for I

How to Treble Your Sales Results in Six Weeks!

know that you will implement everything you are about to learn and I look forward to hearing your success stories.

If you don't believe you can or, if you have doubts about the possibility of trebling your sales results, then before we go any further let's spend some time seeing how we can help you to believe and to gain the attitude of a top performer.

Attributes of a Top Performer

To become a top performer in sales, there are two key factors that you will need. You need '**skill factor**' and you need '**will factor**'. Developing one without the other is like trying to bake a cake and forgetting to add flour. Without flour, a cake will not rise and without the 'will factor' of right attitude and belief, you will never rise to become a top sales performer.

Skill factor is about acquiring the right sales skills and techniques and I teach you lots about these in the coming chapters. I know that unless you develop your 'will factor' first, then reading the rest of this book will simply be a waste of your time. Without the right attitude and belief you will not implement any of the skills and this book will probably become just another volume gathering dust on your desk.

Increasing Your 'Will Factor'

Let's look at a sports analogy as there is a lot of similarity between achieving in sports and achieving in sales. There are sports people who simply do it for a hobby or are semi professional. Then there are those who compete professionally to be the best in their field and achieve their peak performance.

Professionals are consistently striving to be the best. They have a great skill and they become top performers, however, they also possess many different attributes that enable them to develop their skills further so that they remain the best in their field.

A Little Thing That Makes a Big Difference

The attributes that many top sports performers possess are:

- Ability to believe in their success and to be action orientated
- Turn fear into focus
- Take responsibility for their own success
- Inspired by others and willing to learn from former winners
- Take time to develop their skills further and are committed
- Understand what makes them tick and motivates them
- Dedicated and Driven and have the desire to be the best
- Enthusiastic and energetic

Change Your Attitude And Change Your Behaviour

Top performers with the attitude to succeed, display all of these attributes and they consistently develop each and every one of them on a daily basis.

To develop your 'will factor' and think like a top performer you need commitment to developing these attributes on a daily basis so that you can be the best in your field and you can treble your sales results in just six weeks!

Let's see how many of these attributes you already have?

I am going to ask you to imagine a scenario...

- See yourself doing the activity
- Notice what you are saying to yourself
- Notice your attitude
- Notice your physiology

I am going to give you a brand new Ferrari today. The current market value of the Ferrari is £150,000. I haven't got the time or confidence to look for the best price or bargain with dealers... I desperately need to raise £50,000 cash in the next 24 hours so I am going to give it to you today for only £50,000.

You know that, if you can get me the cash today, you can treble your money when you sell the car at full market value tomorrow.

How to Treble Your Sales Results in Six Weeks!

Would you find a way to raise the £50,000 so that you can make a £100,000 profit for yourself immediately after you take it off my hands?

I bet you are saying, "hell yes!!!". This is a quick win and quick way to make £100k profit so only a fool would be saying "no".

Now take yourself through the process of how you would do it. I have added some questions for you consider in your journey.

Your goal is to raise £50k in 24 hours.

- Do you believe you can do it?
- What would it mean to you personally if you make £100k profit immediately?
- What is the first thing you are going to do when you make the £100k profit?
- See yourself doing it? Who is with you and how does it feel?
- How much do you want to achieve this goal?
- What actions would you need to take to make this happen?
- What skills have you already got that would help you?
- What could you do to raise the £50k cash?
- Who would you go to for help?
- Who could you learn from?
- What resources would you use?
- How would you influence others to help you?
- How would you persuade them to give you the capital?
- What barriers are in your way?
- How can you remove these barriers?
- Who is responsible for your success in this task?
- What will you do to ensure that you sustain motivation and your energy?
- How committed are you to achieving success in this task?
- How good do you feel once you have achieved a task

that, when first presented to you, raised many doubts in your mind about your ability to do it and that initially appeared impossible?
- Looking back at your success, what was the one thing that made the biggest difference?.

Congratulations for completing the task successfully! You have just trebled your investment!!!

The bad news is that unfortunately this is only a scenario. However, the good news is that you believed and you achieved. You achieved the task as you ….

- **A**ction orientated and believed in your ability to succeed
- **T**urned fear into focus by removing barriers to your success
- **T**ook responsibility for the task and planned your success
- **I**nstigated a plan and you were committed to it
- **T**asted what success would feel/look/sound like
- **U**sed all of your skills and resources
- **D**ecided on your goals and you were dedicated to achieving it
- **E**nthusiastic and energetic about achieving the task as you could see a real personal benefit from achieving your goals and you wanted it enough!

You have demonstrated that you do have all of the skills to be a top performer. To achieve a similar task in real life, like trebling your sales results in just six weeks, you simply use the same methodology and **you will treble your sales results in six weeks**. In a later chapter, we will create your action plan to achieve it.

So to summarise:

- If you want to treble your sales results in six weeks you need to believe to achieve!
- To build your belief you need to develop the attitude and attributes of a top performer.

How to Treble Your Sales Results in Six Weeks!

Finally, the great thing about your attitude is that you own it. You control it and you choose when to use it. That also means that you choose when to let a bad attitude affect your results.

By changing your attitude, you change your behaviours and by changing your behaviours, you will change your results!

To finish this chapter, let me leave you with a story. It is a children's story that has been told for hundreds of years by Indian chiefs.

They gathered the children around a campfire and told them this: "Children, inside you there is a very big battle that goes on every day. It is the battle of two wolves. One is very fierce and powerful and it is called Limiting Belief. The other is equally as powerful and it is called Empowering Belief. Every day the wolves fight inside you to see which is more powerful and which one can win the battle"

The children listen with anticipation and one little boy, very eager to hear which wolf wins, shoots his hand up in air as high as he can and says, "Chief, Chief, which wolf wins?"

"Ah", said the chief, "well that depends on which one you feed!"

Believe you can treble your sales results in six weeks and you will achieve!

Chapter 2: How & Why Your Prospects Buy

When we buy something, we go through a mental decision process. Whether it is a tube of toothpaste from a supermarket or, deciding what software package is best for our business, we still go through the same process.

Before you argue this does not apply to your industry, let me show you how it does. You see, it doesn't matter whether you are selling to managing directors or 'Joe Public', the fact remains that we all fall into the 'Joe Public' category at some point, as we are all consumers.

Even if you are selling to the MDs at the top, before they make a decision to buy they will still go through the same mental thought process that they would do if they were buying something in their personal life. Therefore, the mental thought process that all prospects go through before making a decision to buy applies to all industries, B2B and B2C sales, field sales and telesales.

The Natural Buyers Transition

Think about the last thing that you bought. Now let's look at the mental process you went through before deciding to buy....

- You may have planned it, or something encouraged you to think about buying it.

How to Treble Your Sales Results in Six Weeks!

- Something about the product or service aroused your interest.
- You started to question what needs you have for it
- You find more information on it.
- You match it to your needs.
- You think about buying.
- You consider the price.
- You consider whether it is worth it and if it is good value.
- Once you decide that the value and gain outweigh the cost and decide that it meets your needs, you buy or invest.

The process you went through before deciding to buy is called, the 'natural buyer's transition' and the great news is that all of your prospects will go through exactly the same process.

How to Help Your Prospects to Buy, Instead of Selling to Them

Who hates feeling that they have been sold to?
The fact is that most of us hate feeling it. As prospects we all want to feel like we are in control, that we got the best deal and that we made a decision to buy rather than being sold to. The same applies to your prospects.

Here is the bit that I am still amazed at … we all know that most prospects hate being sold to, so why do so many sales people still use an approach that actually makes their prospects feel like that?

I meet many sales people and business owners who want to increase their sales results, yet their approach is to talk to as many prospects as possible then overload them with information about their product or service.

With a sales approach like this, I am not surprised that so many sales organisations ask for my help, which of course I am not complaining about as its how I make my living. However, it is certainly not a good approach to take as they are not leading prospects through the natural buying transition. They are using an approach, which will make prospects feel like they are being sold to, which we know they hate.

A much better approach, which gains increased sales, is to stop selling and instead, help your prospects to make a decision to buy.

Telling you to stop selling may sound crazy to some of you reading this, however, let's think about that for a moment. If we all go through the natural buyers' transition surely it makes sense that, when we are trying to get prospects to buy from us, instead of selling to them, we help them by taking them through the buyers' transition, the mental thought process that we all go through before making a decision to buy or invest? To me this is a no brainer!

In order to treble your sales results, you really do need to stop selling products and services and instead create a structured sales process that will take your potential prospects through the natural buyer's transition.

To create a structured sales process simply look at the transition your prospects go through before buying. It should be similar to the one we have just looked at.

Once you have the steps of the buyers' transition you then map a sales step that will take your prospects through the buyer's transition. All of the steps combined will give you your structured sales process.

Example :

Buyers' Transition	**Structured Sales Process**
1. Interest aroused	1. Opening statement
2. Needs appreciated	2. Identify needs
3. Knowledge of the project	3. Gain commitment
4. Suitability appreciated	4. Make the match
5. Price considered	5. Make a recommendation
6. Value appreciated	6. Justify value to price ratio
7. Purchase made	7. Close

Create a Sales Process That Helps Your Prospects to Buy

Having a structured sales process makes a huge difference to you and to your prospects, so it is real win-win to implement one.

From your perspective a structured sales process becomes your 'Sat Nav' in sales. The process takes you step by step to where you need to go which of course is to get a sale. It increases confidence and takes away the panic that many sales people and business owners have when they are unsure of what questions to ask or where to go next in a sales call. It increases your satisfaction and belief in your product or service as, instead of just feeling like you have sold something, you will begin to realise that actually you are really helping prospects. You are either providing them with a gain or reducing or removing a pain.

Although there are so many benefits to using a structured sales process there are many who find it very difficult to do because they have a very bad habit of simply selling and, if they have been making some sales, see no reason to change their approach. However, this does not maximise true sales potential and you are missing many sales opportunities.

From a prospects perspective, a structured sales process that takes them through the buyers' transition is not only refreshing, but it also makes a sales call feel more like a natural conversation.

Put yourself in a prospect's position by thinking about the last time you received a sales call at your home in the evening. How irritated do you get when sales people call you and simply ask if you are the homeowner then trying to flog you a new conservatory or energy saving scheme without even identifying if you have a need for it. Most people get very irritated and either hang up or make up an excuse that they are too busy to talk as they cannot see any value in listening to a tale about something that they don't need.

A 'structured prospect focused sales process' that helps your prospects to make a decision to buy is much more effective as then the flow of your sales call will take your prospects in a direction they are happy with. This makes them much more receptive to taking the call and ultimately to buying.

You now have a structured sales process that will help prospects to buy, so the next step is to have a look at what they will actually be buying from you when they become prospects.

What Are Your Prospects Actually Buying From You?

What do you or your business sell?

If you answered the question by telling me the product or service you are selling, you are making one of the biggest mistakes in sales and you will be very familiar with the feeling of rejection that 'push' sales people experience.

Let me rephrase the question...

What are your prospects actually buying from you?

If your answer is *still* products and services, you are not only losing revenue, your prospects probably feel that you do not understand them so you are probably getting lots of rejections, then your motivation level probably drops dramatically with every call you make.

If your answer this time around was not about your product or service, you are still making a big mistake and losing prospects and revenue. What you are selling and what your prospects are buying, need to be aligned if you want to achieve increased sales results.

Let's look back to the end of the buyers' transition. The final step a prospect goes through before making a decision to buy is 'value appreciated'. Prospects buy when they can see the value add and real personal/business benefits they gain from having your product of service.

Prospects buy value add.

Thinking that your prospects buy products or services is undoubtedly one of the single biggest mistake that sales people make. I see so many sales people and business owners try to sell in this way and then they wonder why they are not hitting their sales targets!

Prospects buy value add, therefore to gain increased sales results, you need to start selling value add.

Selling value add.

Please answer this question immediately and don't think about it….

What is the real value add that your product or services provides?

Did you have to think about it?

If you didn't, great! You are on the right track to gaining increasing sales results.

If you did have to think about it what does that tell you about the sales approach that you have been using and the sales results that you have been achieving?

If you had to think about it, you have probably fallen into the habit of selling products and services. Hopefully you understand by now that you have to get out of this habit as it is damaging your results. What alarms me even more is that if you can't immediately see the value add, [the real business benefits that your product or service provides] then how do you expect your prospects to see it?

20

How & Why Your Prospects Buy

Understanding Value Add

Value add is what prospects gain when they buy your product or service. It is the real benefit. It means something to them that makes a 'real' difference to their everyday life or working day.

Existing prospects are your most valuable source of information as they have already bought your products or services. Therefore to determine the real value add, you simply have to ask your existing prospects what made them buy your product and what is the real benefit they have gained from it.

Once you determine their value add you can then use this to your advantage in order to gain more new business prospects in the future.

How Prospects Perceive Value

How I determine value and how you determine value may be completely different. Likewise, how you perceive value and how your prospects perceive value may also be completely different.

In order to gain increased sales results, it is important to remember this and to understand your prospect's perception of value because you need to be selling what your prospects want to buy and you can only achieve this once you understand how they perceive value.

Prospects want to see that they gain value add and that you are delivering on value before deciding to buy. How do prospects determine if you deliver on value?

Let's consider a product or service that we all use in order to understand how we determine if value is being delivered.

If we look at some key supermarkets we can assess our feelings about how they deliver on value.

The four supermarkets are:
- Asda

How to Treble Your Sales Results in Six Weeks!

- Tesco
- Waitrose
- Marks and Spencers

Which supermarket do you feel delivers value and how did you determine this?

I shop at my local Waitrose as I determine value as 'good quality fresh food'. It is not that I have money growing from trees however, I don't look at the prices each of the supermarkets charge because I don't determine value based on price. I determine value based on the quality I receive.

Some people determine value based on price and some determine value based on what they actually get from the product or service they are buying.

The biggest mistake a sales person can make is presuming that their prospects determine value based on price. For some prospects a lower price can have the opposite effect as people who determine value based on quality can sometimes perceive that the cheapest price reflects inferior quality or the value add.

A good example of this is Marks and Spencer. They had a loyal prospect base with a sound reputation for providing quality foods and clothing although, they have never been the cheapest of stores. Some years ago they fell into financial difficulty. Sales were falling and prospect's perception of the value they delivered was suffering. Younger shoppers felt that M&S had a very 'fuddy duddy' image, which was aimed at the older market.

Their food was perceived as being lovely as a luxury buy for special occasions as opposed to a regular weekly shop. To get them out the financial difficulty they were experiencing they appointed Stuart Rose. His task was to get more prospects through the door and get them to spend more. How did he do it?

Did he lower the price to attract the volume of prospects to Asda and Tesco levels, or did he improve the value perception.?

How & Why Your Prospects Buy

The answer is that he increased prospect's value perception!

He brought in more prospects by introducing new clothing ranges aimed at a younger vibrant market and he stimulated interest by using gorgeous, sexy and fun models such as Mylene Klass and Twiggy in updated advertising campaigns.

He promoted the M&S food brands quality with a clever slogan, 'not just food, this is M&S food.

Stuart Rose knew that his prospects did not determine value based on price, he knew that they determined value based on the quality. He didn't lower the price, instead he increased the value perception and as a result he was even able to increase the prices.

Increase Value And Increase Your Prices

So coming back to how your prospects determine if you deliver on value, some may determine it on what you have to offer and some may determine it based on price. To find out you ask them!! Remember your prospects are your most valuable source of information.

Ask your prospects how they determine value and ask if they feel that you ...

- Exceed on value.
- Deliver value.
- Do not deliver on value.

If you deliver on value you are on the right track. However if you could increase the value, you could increase your prices and increase your prospect spend.

If you are not delivering value you need to increase your value perception that prospects have on your product or service.

If you are exceeding on value then you need to put your

prices up immediately, as it is highly likely that you are undercharging for the value that you deliver and prospects will be willing to pay more as long as you still deliver value.

If you are exceeding in value, increase your prices!

Define your value proposition.

Once you understand your prospect's perception of value, and how they determine value, you can put all of it together to create a solid value proposition that arouses your prospect's interest. Use your value proposition at the start of each call, so that prospects can immediately see the value or real business benefit. Once you have delivered your value proposition, help prospects to buy by taking them through the natural buyers' transition.

Create a Solid Value Proposition

A value proposition is a powerful emotion invoking statement that validates a prospect's unmet need and instils a confidence that their unmet needs will be totally satisfied by you and your business.

It should answer the prospect's question:

Why Should I Buy Your Product/Service?

A Value proposition is not your opinion of what you do, because this is a seller focused solution.

The trick is to translate your view of your offering into one that means something for your target prospects, In other words, *a prospect focused solution.*

A Value proposition should be an encapsulation of ...

- What you do best.
- What you do that is better than your competitors (or

that they don't do at all).
- Something that makes your prospects think… "Yes, that means something to me and could be good for me or my business.

To create your value proposition, consider all of the real benefits prospects get when they buy your product or service. Then look at how you differentiate from others in the markets.

> *"In real estate – location, location, location*
> *In business – Its differentiate, differentiate,*
> *and differentiate"*
> Robert Goizueta, CEO Coca Cola

> *"Differentiate or Die"*
> Jack Trout

You should also include any Unique Selling Propositions [USP] in your value proposition. A USP can include:

- Unique.
- Most experienced.
- Award winning.
- Specialist.
- Expert.
- Only one to offer a guarantee.
- UK's best.
- No 1.
- Oldest.
- Most widely used.
- Offer most choice.

When you have identified what you do best, the real benefits prospects gain, how you differentiate and your USP, you can then create your value proposition and you use the value proposition to arouse your prospect's interest at the start of your sales call.

Chapter 3: Selling is Not Complicated

The Simplicity of Sales

As we discovered in the previous chapter, selling only becomes complicated when poor sales people push products and services. This is a sure fire way to get objections and make your prospects feel like they are being sold to ... which we know they all hate.

To gain increased sales results a better approach is to have a prospect focused sales process that takes your prospects through the natural buyer's transition.

Now I know that a structured sales process makes sense and I know that it works as I have trained thousands of sales people to use it and they have all gained increased sales results. However, there will be some of you that look at the all of the steps and think. where do I sell and when can I get to the close?

I meet thousands of sales people and business owners in my seminars and it is guaranteed that I always get at least one sales person come and ask me **"What is the secret to closing more new business?"**

Perfect Your Opening And The Close Happens Naturally

How to Treble Your Sales Results in Six Weeks!

There is no secret in the closing.The real secret is to perfect your opening. When you perfect your opening, you will find that the close happens naturally and in some cases, you will be in the very fortunate position of having prospects asking you to take their order instead of you having to do a hard close.

If you cannot wait to start talking about your products and you are dying to go for the close I need you to lose one thing. Lose your EGO!!

Loose your Ego!

The sale isn't about you, it is about understanding what prospects see as value add. It is about how your solutions can add value and it is about helping your prospects to buy. The sooner you realise this and the sooner you lose your ego, the sooner you will treble your sales results in just six weeks.

Selling is simply asking....

- The right people.
- The right questions.
- The right time.
- The right solution.

Identify Your Key Decision Makers

So we are now ready to start making the sales call which is going to help your prospects to buy!

The first thing to do is check that you are talking to the right person. The right person to speak to is the key decision maker, whether that is the homeowner or the managing director of a business.

Whatever you do, please do not continue with the sales call until you have clarified that you are talking to the right person. Otherwise you may go the whole way through the sales process to discover that they loved the sound of your product or service although they are not the person you need to speak to. Not checking this vital first step can be such a time waster, as you then have to pitch your solution multiple times.

Whether you are in B2B or B2C sales, the only person you need to speak to is the one who is able to influence the decision and has the authority to pull the strings, control the budget or spend the money.

To identify the key decision maker, just ask who is responsible for making the decision on gaining the value add you will be providing.

For example, I would ask, *"Who is the person that makes the decision on selecting a training programme that will deliver up to a 400% increase in your sales results?"*

The increase in sales results is the real value add that my potential prospects are looking for and I have asked for the person who makes the decision on it. All you have to do is the same.

If somebody tells you they are involved in the decision, it is wise to ask how they influence the decision and who has the final say. If they do indeed highly influence the decision then I would ask for a meeting with all parties involved to ensure meeting everybody's needs before recommending a solution.

Deliver an Opening Statement That Grabs Your Prospects Attention

The first step in the buyers' transition is to arouse the prospects interest. We have already established that it is real value add that arouses a prospects interest therefore your first step in the sales process is to deliver a strong opening statement that grabs your prospect's attention. You have already created your value proposition in the previous chapter.

Along with your value proposition a strong opening statement should include:

Who you are.

- This is easy as it is simply your name.

Where you are from.

- This is the business name, however don't just say the business name and expect them to know who you are. Instead, you need to build up the credibility of the business name so that your prospect can identify with it. To build credibility in your business name you can include some of the USPs that you identified in the last section such as 'The UK's No.1 provider'. You can also include names of famous people, brands or businesses that you currently supply and that your prospects will relate to.

Why you are calling.

- This is where you present a valid reason for the call.

What's in it for your prospect.

- This is the most important part and where you deliver the value add that they will gain from having your product or service. If a prospect can not see that there is a personal gain or real business benefit in it for them to take your call then you will get lots of 'I am too busy' or 'not interested', which is why this is the most important part of the introduction.

What's' in it for them should clearly state what your prospects want to hear. It is the true value add that your prospects gain by buying your product or service.

When you combine the who, where, why and what's in it for them you have a very strong opening statement that will grab your prospects attention and arouse their interest.

Selling is Not Complicated

A strong opening statement includes the real value add.

After delivering your opening statement you then need to develop a dialogue with your prospects which you can do with an opening question.

The objective of using an open question at this point is to gain a rapport building response from your prospect and then go into the next step of the sales process which is identifying their needs. A good open question should gain a factual answer and it should also be relevant to your prospect.

Bad opening questions, which I have heard a lot of, are:

• *"How are you today?"* Why is bad? Well firstly, you don't know the prospect personally and really it is none of your business how they are. Secondly, what are you going to do if they say they are having a terrible day!

• *"Have you heard of us?"* Why is that bad? Firstly, it makes you sound weak. Secondly, you have just built up the credibility of the company and delivered a strong what's in it for them. If the answer is that they have never heard of you, you have just lost that credibility.

Good opening questions are:

• *"How did you enjoy the exhibition?"* (If it was an exhibition where you met them)

• *"John Smith tells you are the person to speak to, Is that right?"*

These questions are much better as the gain a factual answer and open up the dialogue between you and the prospect.

How to Effectively Handle Early Objections

'Early' is the operative word here!!

The biggest mistake you can make with early objections is to answer them! Because they are not real!

The reason prospects give you early objections is quite simply because you have not delivered a strong enough introduction and you have not grabbed their attention. By answering at this early stage there is only one way the call can go and that is to confrontation, then the prospect loses all interest in listening to you.

Instead of attempting to answer a false early objection you should agree with it and go back into your introduction again so that your prospect can clearly see that there is a real benefit in them taking your call.

At this stage of any sales call it is imperative that you avoid confrontation as you need your prospect to be open with you if you are to identify all of their needs, and you don't get an open mind when a prospect feels that you are being confrontational.

Identify your prospect's needs.

When you stop selling products and services – PUSH.
When you start establishing your prospects needs - PULL.

This is when you will start to see a dramatic increase in your sales results!!!!

Imagine this scenario. You go to see your doctor and you say that you are in pain. Before even asking you about your illness or the pain, they write you a prescription and tell to just take it and it will help you.

How would you feel? Would you have confidence in the doctor, would you be happy to take the prescription without them asking anything about your illness and would you use that doctor again? The answer is no! If a doctor gave you a prescription without diagnosing your illness first they could be struck off for malpractice.

"Prescription before diagnosis is malpractice!"

The same theory applies to sales, if you don't ask the right questions to identify a prospects needs then you cannot confidently recommend a product or solution to meet their needs. Poor sales people push products! Great sales people pull out prospect needs first, then they help the prospects to make the match between their needs and your offers and they ensure that resolving their needs outweighs the cost of your solution. By pushing products you are pushing your prospects away and probably into the hands of your competitors, therefore lets look at how you can pull out a prospect's needs.

Adopting a pull mentality.

In order to adopt a pull mentality you need to develop your questioning techniques. Establishing needs is all about asking the right prospects the right questions at the right time. However, before you start asking loads of questions it is better to explain to them that you are going to ask some questions to identify their needs so that you can both focus on finding the right solutions. By explaining this upfront, your prospects will not feel like you are interrogating them and they will be more receptive to your questions.

There are two key types of needs that prospects have. They either have a pain that they need you to reduce or remove or, they need you to show them a gain or real business benefit.

Your prospects will always do more to avoid pain than they will to gain pleasure so 'Pull out the Pain first !!!'

Pull out the pain first !!!

How to Treble Your Sales Results in Six Weeks!

To help you identify potential pain, complete the following exercise:

1. Make a list of all of the benefits/gain your prospects get from your products/services.
2. Write down all of the benefits/gain that your product or service solves.
3. Next, re-engineer those benefits into pain! Spell out what your prospects situation would be if they don't use your product or service.

Then, your next step is to create a set of killer sales questions that will identify every need.

If you have already spent some time in sales you will know by now that the only type of questions you should be asking are open questions!

Open questions get the prospects talking and when they are talking you can listen out for their needs.

Your job is to ask the right questions and let the prospects talk. Listening at this stage is key as when you actively listen you establish the right needs, the importance of the need and also by listening actively you won't have to think about questions you should ask next.

As a rule of thumb, open questions should always start with who, why, what , why , when and how. 'Tell me' is also a great way to start a question as it is very open and encourages the prospect to talk about themselves or their business.

Do not make the mistake of selling your products or services to the first need you hear! Instead complete all of the questions so that you can identify enough of the right needs!

20 Killer Sales Questions

To effectively gain all of the needs there a series of questions that I recommend you use:

Selling is Not Complicated

- Qualifying questions.
- Pain inducing questions.
- Payoff questions.
- Feedback questions.

Qualifying questions.

Qualifying questions are used to gain some background information and open up the conversation. Depending on when and where your lead came from will determine how many qualifying questions you will need to ask. Qualifying questions could include:

- Who they are.
- How they heard about you.
- Why they made the initial enquiry.
- Their understanding of what you do.
- What sort of timeframe they are looking at?
- Have they looked at any competitors?
- How long they have been looking for a solution?
- What are their reasons for looking for a solution?
- What attracted them to your lead generation method?
- What are your must have's?
- What are your nice to haves?
- What long term/short term results are you looking for?

To create your set of qualifying questions simply review some of your recent customers or recent sales and decide on the key things that you need to qualify in advance.

Create a set of key qualifying questions:
1.

2.

3.

4.

5.

Pain inducing questions.

The most powerful questions of all!

In the earlier exercise, you re-engineered the benefits your product or service provides to create a set of pain inducing questions. Simply refer back to the earlier exercise and using the open questioning rules create a set of five pain inducing questions to elicit a prospect's problem or pain.

Some example of pain inducing questions:

- What are the key challenges you face today?
- How important is….?
- How many more enquiries would you really need?
- What are the consequences of not getting this?
- How does that affect you….?
- What you like to happen…..?
- How do you deal with that……?

Create a set of pain inducing/problem questions:
1.

2.

```
3.



4.



5.


```

The trick with pain inducing questions is to identify the 'real' pain and how much it means to them or would cost them if they don't have a solution place.

By establishing the consequences or the cost you equip yourself with the knowledge that will be extremely powerful if they try to batter you down on price. When it gets to the close you are armed with the right information to show them how the value they are getting from solution outweighs the cost.

Gain the right information to show that value outweighs the price.

Payoff questions.

This is the clever part. You have just asked pain inducing questions to identify all of the problems or challenges your prospects are facing so next we ask about the gain they would get by reducing or removing or that pain. By firstly asking about pain then asking your prospects to tell you the gain they would receive, they are now starting to make the match between their problems and your suitable solution.

How to Treble Your Sales Results in Six Weeks!

By asking the right questions you will get your prospect to do the selling themselves. This means you don't have to sell, all you have to do is ask the right questions to help your prospects buy.

Good payoff questions would be:

- What would it mean for your business if?
- What is the biggest gain you would like to receive and what would it mean to you?
- What are the financial benefits if...?
- What are the benefits of sorting out ...?
- What is the payback of dealing with ...?
- How will it feel once you have this sorted?

Create a set of Payoff questions :

1.

2.

3.

4.

5.

Selling is Not Complicated

Feedback questions.

Finally we have, feedback questions. Feedback questions are designed to make sure that you are going along the right track with your prospect. They can be used as trial close questions to check that your prospect can understand the value add that you have so far described. They can check the prospects willingness to place an order and they can also pull out any underlying objections that the prospect may be thinking of. Always ask feedback questions before going to the next step so that you are prepared in advance.

Good feedback questions are:

- So if you could have a solution that does ...... would that be of interest to you?
- Does this look good to you?
- Am I along the right track?
- Does this look like something that would work for you?
- How do you feel about this?
- Is this along the right lines for you?
- Does this look like something that you could use?

If the prospect gives you positive feedback then great!

If not, you need to isolate the reasons why and get back on track.

Create five feedback questions:
1.

2.

3.

4.

5.

Summary.

To successfully identify a prospect's needs you follow these steps. Then you can then match your product or service to meet your prospect's needs.

- Qualify
- Pull out the Pain first !!!
- Adopt a "pull" rather than a "push" mentality
- If you push benefits you will lose interest
- Identify the benefits/gain your prospect wants to have
- Feedback questions
- Next we gain commitment and then solve their pain, problem or needs with what you have to offer.

Gain Your Prospects Commitment

Before you start to make the match with your product or service always check if you have gained *all* of the prospect's needs. This will prevent sales objections at the end of the call and gives you the opportunity to check that you have heard everything correctly.

Simply explain that you would like to check that you have gained all of the relevant information and that you have understood their needs correctly. Then repeat back everything they have told you.

At this stage, I would also ask if there are any other needs they have and which you have not yet discussed.

Chapter 4: Sell Value Instead of Price

You can now start to sell your solution.

The secret is not in how you sell or how you close, the secret is to perfect your opening!

If you have successfully followed all of the steps and advice I have given you, your prospects will have already started to sell your solution to themselves. Let's review what has happened from their perspective so far....

⇨ They have heard a strong value proposition and can see that there is a valid reason to listen to you – Value add.

⇨ Unlike most sales people who simply push products you have explained that before recommending any solution you need to establish more about their needs – very refreshing for them !

⇨ You have asked a series of questions that have enabled them to openly tell you about the current challenges and pain that they have. You then asked a set of payoff questions and your prospects have openly told you that there are many benefits to them having a solution that removes or reduces their pain – this is where the prospect start to weigh up the problem versus the solution.

How to Treble Your Sales Results in Six Weeks!

⇨You have asked some feedback questions to check you are both on the same track – This confirms that you can move forward in the sale.

⇨You have clarified that you have gained all of your prospect's needs. You have checked that you have understood them correctly and repeated them back to affirm that they do have a need for your solution.

Match Your Solution to Meet Your Prospect's Needs

You now need to match your solution to your prospect's needs and show them how your solution meets these.

The trick to selling your solution is that you don't undersell and you don't oversell. To successfully sell your solution you simply need to repeat each need and then show them how your solutions meet them.

What you don't want to do, at this stage, is start to sell all of the 'bells and whistles' of your solution. By doing so you could oversell your solution to them which can result in objections at the end, Your prospect may only be interested in 50% of what your solution has to offer and therefore they may object to paying full price for only using half of the benefits your solutions provides.

Selling your solution should not be about cost. It must be about how you can meet their needs and how you can add value.

Sell Value – Not price.

Make a Recommendation And Help Your Prospects to Buy

Once you have shown how your solution can meet their needs you then need to make a recommendation on the actual solution you can offer.

Sell Value Instead of Price

In the recommendation you need to include:

- Quantity.
- Price.
- Timeframe.

You need to justify why you have made the recommendation as this helps the prospects to justify that they do get value add.

You also need to quantify that the value they gain from having your solution outweigh any cost.

Do not be tempted to sell on price!

This is a good time in the sales process to use testimonials from other prospects so that you can have some social proof from a similar customer as proof that you do indeed provide the value add you are claiming.

How Prospects Justify Their Decision to Buy

Justify value versus price.

Sell on value – not on price. Prospects buy when they can see that they are going to gain value add from your product or service; they also need to weigh up the price. When the value add outweighs the cost, then this is when they buy. Your final step of the sale, before the close, is to help your prospects understand that the value really does outweigh the cost!

So how do we justify value? Well its simple. You back up through their pain and challenges which you have already identified and you show them the gain they would like to get. Once you have the pain and the gain and you have demonstrated that your product or service provide a solution you should go a step further by establishing what it means to them personally if they find a solution. The operative word here is 'personal'.

When prospects make a decision to buy there is always an

emotional reason why they do so. When prospects do buy they don't justify their purchase emotionally, they justify it rationally!

Let me give you an example, which is actually a true story, to help you understand.

In 2003 my husband and I were buying a new car. I wanted to buy a Porsche and he wanted to buy a Lotus. My dream of having a Porsche went out the window after discovering I was pregnant with our first child, which we were thrilled about. So instead of buying a nice sports car we had to start looking for a family car, so we went to Mercedes Benz to look at a more suitable vehicle.

However, my husband *really* wanted a Lotus and could not give up on his dream. Although we had discussed it and had agreed that we were not getting a Lotus my husband went ahead and bought it anyway! Believe me I was not very happy when I heard it roaring up my driveway and he was in big trouble with me for ignoring our agreement!

So after making a very noisy entrance my husband knew he had to face the music and justify his actions to me before I hit the roof!

So how do you think he justified his decision, did he justify it emotionally or rationally?

Let's look at the emotional reasons why my now ex husband bought the Lotus.......

Emotional buying needs.

- Ego.
- His last chance to own one before kids.
- He always dreamed of having one.
- Its easier to ask for forgiveness than permission.
- He wanted to feel good driving in it.
- He wanted to have a better car than his friends.
- He felt the need for speed.
- He wanted a 'boy's toy'.

All of the above reasons are actually why he bought the car.

Sell Value Instead of Price

However, you can imagine my response if he had of come home and justified his purchase to me by using the above reasons. He actually bought the car emotionally, like all customers, he bought emotionally but justified rationally.

He was actually very clever in how he justified his buy and he managed to convince us both that the value he received from car outweighed the £23 000 price tag and that he had good justification to make his purchase!

So here is his rational justification: By the time our son was born a family car like the Mercedes would have depreciated in value considerably. However as a Lotus actually retains it value and he was planning to do some extra work on the car himself he could make a profit nine months later, which we could then use to upgrade to a higher specification Mercedes.

Great justification, don't you think? I have to say I was very impressed with it and it did make sense as we weren't losing any money, in fact we were going to make more. So, even though I know he bought it emotionally, he justified his decision to buy to me rationally. Your prospects will also do this before they give you an order.

Therefore you need to pull out your prospect's emotional and rational buying needs so that we can enable them to justify that the value add they gain outweighs the cost of the solution.

An example of emotional buying needs, which often dominate the decision, are:

- Hassle factors.
- Stress.
- Best choice.
- Makes their life easier.
- Makes their jobs easier.
- They want to be the best.
- They really want it.
- Ego.
- They have always dreamed of having your solution.

How to Treble Your Sales Results in Six Weeks!

As emotional needs are based on a feeling, ask your prospects to tell you their emotional needs, *"How will you feel when we remove or reduce the current pain you have or get the gain?"* Once they start to open up and tell you how it will make them feel, you can follow it by asking, *"What will solving this or gaining this mean to you **personally?**"*

So now that you have the emotional needs, your next step is to help your prospects justify their decision. To justify their decision remember you need to pull the rational needs.

Prospects generally rationalise their decision based on either time or money:

- They save time.
- They make time.
- They save money.
- They make money.

Time and money are great ways for prospects to justify their decisions and even though it is not their key reasons for buying we know that they will use time or money to justify to themselves and others, the rationale behind making their decision to buy.

Let us use my business as an example. By making a decision to invest in my training programmes my prospects:

- Save time – as I remove underperformance from their sales teams.
- Make time – to gain more sales as I remove the non sales related activities.
- Save money – as they are currently losing money by not achieving peak performance now.
- Make money – they make a lot more money as, by providing sales people with the selling skills, techniques and tools they sell to more prospects as well as increasing the value and profit of each purchase.

Sell Value Instead of Price

All of the above are rational buying needs and how prospects justify their decision to invest in me. So, by having your product or service how can your prospects justify their decision rationally?

By understanding the emotional and rational buying needs of your prospects you can then ask them the right question to enable to them justify their decision to themselves. In the box below make a note of your prospects emotional and rational buying needs:

Emotional	Rational

Next create a set of questions that you can ask your prospects to get them to justify their decision rationally and help them to understand that they value does outweigh the cost.

Create a set of questions that will help to identify emotional buying needs and how your prospects could rationally justify their decision to buy.

1.

2.

3.

4.

5.

Make it easy for your prospects to buy from you.

Once you have helped the prospects to rationalise their decision you need to make it easy for them to buy from you.

This means you need to tell them exactly how they can buy, when they can buy and the next step they need to take which will lead you nicely into the close.

How they can buy, when they can buy and the next step.

Sell Value Instead of Price

- How they buy – do they have to raise a purchase order, do they have to order in advance and if so when will they receive it?
- When they buy – It is important at this point that you get prospects to act quickly and that you do not give them a chance to talk themselves out of the sale so do NOT offer to send information as this could delay their decision. Instead explain to the prospect that now is the time to buy and to strike whilst the iron is hot.
- The next step – explain the very next step they have to take to receive the value add and then ask your closing question.

You need to tell your prospects exactly how they can buy from you and make it easy for them. If you leave unanswered questions at this stage you will be inviting objections and raising questions or doubts about the rational decision they are about to make. Do not leave any stone unturned or allow the prospects to have any unanswered questions in their head before going for the close!

Have The Confidence to Ask For The Order

The Close.

You have completed all of the steps of the sales and have successfully taken your prospect through the natural buyer's transition so the last step is to ask for the order, if your prospect has not already 'closed' for themselves.

You have just helped the prospect to justify their decision in the previous step therefore all that is left for you to do at this stage is ask the closing question.

When delivering your closing question you ask _and then you SHUT UP!_

Say it and Shut up!

How to Treble Your Sales Results in Six Weeks!

By shutting up you allow the prospects to go through the natural buyers' transition and tick all of the boxes that they need to mentally visit before giving you a yes!

Interrupting with more questions means you interrupt the prospect's thought process and can make them uncertain as to whether all of the boxes have been ticked or not.

Prospects will go silent after you ask the close question. Good sales people understand that prospects need to mentally justify their decision and the silence is simply thinking time.

Poor sales people cannot bear the silence and feel like they need to keep talking … which could mean they unintentionally talk the prospect out of the sale.

To increase your confidence I suggest that you stand up to deliver a confident close question and, that you keep a copy of the buyers' transition in front of you to remind yourself that your prospects are simply going through the mental thought process and ticking the boxes.

Once you have delivered the close question, the prospects will go one of three ways:

- They agree and take your product or service.
- They want to negotiate.
- They have an objection.

When prospects say yes!

Congratulations, you have just got a sale! You have taken your prospect through the natural buyers' transition and they have rationally justified their purchase and decided to spend their money with you. Your prospect is now a customer. They get value add and you get your commission.

Remember at the start we said that people hate being sold to! Prospects want to feel that they are in control and that they are making a decision to buy.

Although you have taken your prospect through the natural buyers' transition, at this stage there will always be a few of them who feel like they need to trade or negotiate with you, so that they can feel that they retain the control in the sale.

When this happens, keep a couple of things in mind.

Knowing When to Negotiate And When to Trade

The Rules for negotiating.

- Never give without getting something in return.
- Trade one thing at a time.

If you offer something, before gaining their commitment to go ahead, you run a huge risk of the prospect taking advantage of you. As an example, if you give prospects a 10% discount without gaining commitment they know they are in control, that you will give in to them and will therefore keep asking your for more and more discount until you break.

If you give an inch some prospects will take a mile!

When prospects do want to negotiate with you always stay in control by telling them what you need in return before negotiating with them.

The right way to achieve this is by saying …
The right way… "If you … then I?"

This is assertive and gains their commitment before offering your suggestion.

The wrong way to achieve this is by saying...
The wrong way … "If I … would you?"

This sounds weak and is opening the floodgates for your prospects to take advantage of your suggestions. Remember no commitment means no order!

What can you negotiate with?

Prospects who like to negotiate need to feel they have gained control with something additional to the product or service offered.

They love freebies, discount, and any variables that you can add to the sale. Prepare for your prospects to negotiate with you and have a list of variables to hand that you can use to negotiate with so that when you are on the call you are ready and confident to win the negotiation.

How to Deal With Objections

In an ideal world all prospects will say 'yes'. If for some reason you are not talking to the right types of prospects or, if you haven't followed all of the steps of the sale in the right order, you may get an objection.

To successfully handle these objections you need to bear a few things in mind:

- An objection is simply your prospects way of explaining that they need more help to justify their decision.
- An objection is not a NO, so don't give in as soon as you get one.
- Many objections that prospects give you are FALSE.

As a sales person the rule to successfully handle objections is to stay in control, do not lose confidence, avoid confrontation and identify if the objections are actually real before you start to answer them.

This is where poor sales people lose. As soon as they hear the objection it hurts their ego and, instead of dealing with each objection confidently and moving on, the ego stricken sales person argues their case with the hope that they prospects will back down and agree with them. They won't!

Good sales people understand that confrontation is not good. They avoid confrontation by listening to their prospects objections, they repeat back to them so that their prospects can see that they are showing empathy, they have listened to them and they have understood their objection. By simply showing some empathy and letting the prospects know that you have heard them they will be more open and receptive to hearing your answer.

However, before answering objections', always check if they are real and if they are any other objections.

To identify if the objection is 'REAL' simply ask your prospects to tell you exactly what they mean by their objection.

By asking them to explain more you will be able to get more details on the objection so that you can identify the real one.

A good example of this is a money objection. Let's say the objection is that your product or service is too expensive.

Poor sales people automatically think this means that the prospect doesn't have any money. However 'too expensive' could mean loads of things. It could mean:

- They cannot see that the value outweighs the cost.
- It is simply too expensive right now but maybe not in the future.
- It is more expensive than your competitors.
- They have seen your product or service cheaper some where else.

'Too expensive' could have so many different meanings so by answering what you *think* it means instead of clarifying the meaning with your prospects will only lead to MORE OBJECTIONS. To prevent this simply ask your prospects *exactly* what they mean.

Before answering, check if this is the only objection they have. Always check first otherwise you could answer one objection only to discover that there are three more waiting for you.

Once you have clarified what they mean and that this is the only objection, go for the close.

How to answer objections.

Prospects need to feel that you understand their objection; they need to know that they are not alone in having it and they need to hear that other customers who had a similar objection found a way to overcome it. A very effective process to answer objections, which is a very old one but a great one that and I have been successfully using for over 15 years, is the '3 F's Formula'.

The formula is: FEEL, FELT, FOUND. However you must bear in mind that for this formula to be truly effective you MUST also follow what we covered on the previous page which is you must firstly check if the objection is real, secondly clarify exactly what your prospects means and then thirdly you check it is the ONLY objection they have before using the 3 F's formula to answer!

Feel – I understand how you feel.
Felt – Other prospects have felt like that.
Found – However, what they found...

The first F – Feel, ensure the prospects that there will be no confrontation and that you empathise with their objection.

The second F – Felt, ensure that they don't feel alone or it is not unreasonable for them to have this objection.

The third F – Found, helps them to see that there are others who had similar objections and you found them a solution and now those customers are receiving the value add that your product or service provides.

Existing customers are great social proof that you do deliver value add and that you have found solutions for other prospects in the past, therefore in the third F-stage use as many existing scenarios or testimonials as possible to help you overcome objections.

If you feel that to answer the objection you may need to trade or negotiate, you still need to follow the rules for

Sell Value Instead of Price

trading that we cover earlier. So, as an example, if the objection was 'too expensive', explain how another customer split the cost into monthly payments. Don't just go straight in an offer monthly payments, instead you explain that if they give you an order that you *may* be able to offer the same and you close them again.

This is a very simple yet very effective process for answering real objections and it works! So next time you get objections, give it a try and watch how many prospects that you may have previously walked away from, Buy and become customers.

Golden Rules of Closing

- Before closing you must determine the prospects needs.
- You must be able to identify that the needs outweigh the cost.
- Ask the question and then be quiet – the silence is just the prospect thinking about his decision.
- Stay in control.
- Listen to the prospect.
- Only answer objections when you have checked if it is the real and the *only* objection they have.
- Avoid confrontation.
- Never give without getting something in return.
- Trade one thing at a time.
- Never over or under-estimate prospects.
- Show empathy, not sympathy.
- Rehearse it!

You have now successfully created a structured sales process. To ensure it enables you to treble your sales results in six weeks you now need to do the most important part. This to implement it and create a strategy that will enable you to treble your sales results!

Chapter 5: Identify Your Revenue Tap & Turn it on!

Planning is a huge contributing factor to sales success. People who take the time to plan their sales approach understand that selling is not about picking the phone up as many times as you can and speaking to as many people as you can. It is about planning to speak to the **right prospects**, at the right time and, asking them the right questions so that you can present the right solutions to meet their needs.

Get Out of The Habit of *"If I call enough prospects some will buy."*

When I first started working in sales my friends and family all thought that it would be a very hard job as they imagined that there would be loads of sales people constantly picking up the phone to anyone who would listen, and trying to flog them some products and services.

Sales for some organisations can be like this where staff are like battery hens and they just keep calling and calling anyone who will listen to them. This is very hard work that delivers poor results! Calling as many prospects as possible is not a smart strategy to have. Many companies now understand that, to achieve a higher level of sales success, a much smarter approach is needed so that sales people can talk to more of the right prospects rather than just more people.

How to Treble Your Sales Results in Six Weeks!

Talk to more of the right prospects rather than more people.

To treble your sales results you need to get out of the habit of *"If I call enough people some will buy,"* and instead, create a strategic plan to call more of the right prospects so that you have a strong opportunity to make a sale on each call.

Identifying the right prospect target market is a key contributor to your success and should be the first thing to identify in your plan.

To identify your target market you can:

- Look at back which industries or prospects have previously bought your products or services.
- Look at your competitors' websites to identify the type of customers that buy from them
- Look at all of the pain you identified that your product or service reduces or removes, and ask yourself which industries / sectors or prospects base could be experiencing some of the same pain or problems.
- Look at all of the gain you identified and again ask yourself which industries / sectors or prospects base could welcome some of the gains you delivered.

Once you have identified your target market you can create a penetration matrix that will segment your prospect base into categories that will enable you to call the prospects with most potential and take them to a close in the next six weeks.

Identify your revenue tap and turn it on!

There are two main ways to gain increased revenue in the next six weeks. You have your existing customers that could potentially spend more with you and, you have new business prospects.

Generally, because new business takes a lot longer to close, it can sometimes be easier to get more revenue from your existing prospects. I am not saying that you should not focus time on generating new business; instead, I am saying that you need to identify all possible revenue streams and identify the revenue tap you can turn on that will generate revenue and close within the next six weeks.

If you have identified that the revenue tap to turn on is your existing prospect base then the first step is to review all existing accounts. In these account reviews what you are really trying to identify is:

- The last time you had contact with each customer.
- Each customer's real business needs.
- The pain or gain they currently have.
- Which products/services you have that will match their needs.
- Which products/services they have already purchased.
- Which additional products/services you have that will also meet their needs.
- What would encourage them to spend additional money in the next six weeks.
- What actions could you take that would enable you to gain more up sell or additional revenue from these sources in the next six weeks.

If the revenue tap that you can turn on is new business then I would suggest that you identify the following:

- The industries/markets that have the biggest GAIN from your products/services.
- The industries/markets that have the biggest PAIN, which your products/services can remove or reduce.
- The industries that are not spending money at the moment.
- The industries or prospects who have seen the most 'value add' from your products and services.
- The competitors of your existing prospects who are already using your products or services and have seen success from using them.

How to Treble Your Sales Results in Six Weeks!

This may take you some time to do however, it is time well spent! A coach once told me "there are times when you have to go slow, in order to go faster", and in this case, it is very true. Take the time out to plan a strategic approach, identify your target market, and create a plan and the increased sales results will happen much quicker than easier than if you were to simply continue working hard.

Create a Prospect Penetration Matrix

Once you have identified your revenue tap you can then segment your target market by providing each account with a status so that you can flag prospects with the highest potential and call them first.

An easy and logical way to split your prospect base is to have a traffic light system to contacting your prospects base. Identifying your accounts Red, Amber or Green (RAG) status

Red accounts:

- Customers who simply repeat the same order every month.
- Customers who have a contract with you.
- Customers who you know will not be placing further orders this year.
- Accounts/industries that you know are not buying at the moment.

Amber accounts:

- Accounts that are stuck in your pipeline.
- Contracts that are due to come to an end.
- Dormant accounts that you could win back.
- Accounts/Industries that **may be** affected by a recent change.
- Accounts/Industries that you could develop further.

Identify Your Revenue Tap & Turn it on!

Green Accounts:

- Quick Win or a visible opportunity.
- Accounts in your pipeline that are forecasted to close by the end of your six week period.
- Current accounts that have a current pain/gain that can be influenced by external sources.
- Accounts/Industries that you know are affected by a recent change.
- Accounts where you can sell additional products/services.
- Accounts that a current offer may influence to buy.

In the next six weeks Red accounts have the least opportunity, so remove them from your call/contact list as they have the lowest current potential.

Amber accounts should be on your call/contact list as there is a potential in each of them. The objective of working the amber accounts is to move them into red or into green once. As Amber accounts may take longer to close, call them first, followed by the green accounts.

Identify External Influences That Could Increase Sales Results

It is important to remember that even though you may feel you know your prospect's needs, there are many external sources that can increase a prospect's need or pain/gain to buy your products or that could effect the status of your accounts.

Imagine that you sell food ingredients and some of the major supermarkets introduced changes to their stock lists that would eliminate some products. This decision to change is outside of both you and your customers' control. It is an external influence that may have a major effect on the buying and selling situation. If you have, an alternative and you can identify prospects that may be affected by this then you have just added many green, visible opportunities to your pipeline.

Example:

Pain
Sainsbury's have withdrawn all products with monosodium glutamate. (MSG)
Gain
You can now approach those suppliers and sell an MSG replacement which you stock.

External influences can really help you to build you sales pipeline look out for industry specific news that may present you with an opportunity to sell to prospects that have previously said no.

Identify Offers That Can Influence Prospects to Buy

Sometimes prospects will still buy even if they don't have a need.

Even if prospects have said no to you before that does not necessarily mean that they will never buy, as sometimes they can be influenced, even if they have told you previously that they don't need your product or service.

Prospects can be influenced to buy by:

- A sale that is on for a limited time period.
- A special offer.
- A unique opportunity.
- A saving.
- An offer.

Therefore, in your planning stage you need to indentify your account status, external influences that may affect some of your target market and any incentives or offers that may influence prospects to buy. Once you have identified all of this you now have a targeted prospect list to call or visit.

Ask for referrals

Referrals are the best sales lead you can get so when you make the calls to everyone on your new list, ask them for the names and numbers of other friends and colleagues that may also be interested in gaining the value add that you provide.

Chapter 6: Gaining Increased Focus & Momentum

Calling prospects at the right time – your prime selling time.

In sales it is simple, the more right prospects you talk to, the more likely it will be that you will hit target and achieve increased sales results. For me this is a no brainer, however I see many sales people that are actually spending a lot of their time on non sales related activities and in the prime business/selling hours they are doing admin instead of calling the people who can help them to hit target; their prospects.

This is one of the first areas I examine when I visit sales organisations to help them increase their sales results. I observe the sales teams, I sit side by side with them to see what activities they are doing and I listen in to prospect calls to establish how effectively they are using their time and to see if they are they making the most of what I call 'prime selling time'.

The Importance of Productivity

I ask the sales people to show me their 'To do List' for the day. I then go through each item and ask them…

⇨Why is this task important for you to do today?
⇨How will it help you to achieve your goals and target?

How to Treble Your Sales Results in Six Weeks!

⇨What is the benefit of taking this action today?
⇨What time are you planning to take this action at today?
⇨What is the consequence of you not taking this action?
⇨How long have you had this on your to do list for?

I promise you, you would be amazed at the results I get. Approximately, 30% of what is on their list is sales related and in prime selling time, and the other 70% is simply keeping them busy.

This means that a lot of sales team are only using 30% of their efforts and their time in activities that will enable them to gain increased sales results.

Having been in sales for many years, of course I understand that admin is a necessary evil and that some is to complete orders. The key to gaining increased sales results is to ensure that you separate the admin time from the prime selling time.

In every sales team I have run, I have always introduced a prime selling time, so it was no surprise that my team won the awards for best call times, best target achievement and best new business team. The way I look at it is; if prospects are more available in specific hours during the day, it makes good business sense for sales people to call then and to do admin in the times when prospects are generally too busy or not receptive to taking calls.

Introducing a prime selling time and separating call time from admin time is by far the best thing you can do to improve your effectiveness as a sales person and to gain increased sales results.

Introducing a Prime Selling Time

To introduce a prime selling time, I would recommend the following:

• 9am – 9.30am: Admin.

Gaining Increased Focus & Momentum

- **9.30am – 12.00pm: Prime selling time.**
- 12pm - 1pm: Lunch.
- 1pm -2pm: Admin.
- **2pm - 4.30pm: Prime selling time**.
- 4.30pm – 5.30pm: Admin.

During prime selling time you need to spend your time talking to prospects and ignoring emails and distractions. The increase in your productivity and sales results will eventually help you to see that making more calls makes you more money and gets you closer to achieving your personal goals.

In terms of targets for each day I would highly recommend that you set a target of making 70 telesales calls a day and 12 prospect appointments in field sales, as not all of your prospects will be available to speak to you. I would also suggest that at least three hours of your day is spent on prospect talk time which means in an actual sales pitch with your prospects or customers.

Productivity = Profitability

Remove Non Sales Related Activities

Removing time thieves in your way:

List all of the non-sales activities that are currently getting in your way of selling.

Daily	Weekly	Monthly

Next I would like you to highlight all of those activities that are still very important and urgent and that still need to be done.

Out of those activities that you still need to do what time do you need to do them at? If they are in your prime selling hours what can you do in order to complete them outside the prime selling time.

Identify all of the activities that are not both urgent and important and take them off your list and delegate them to another non-sales related person in the team.

Gain Increased Focus And Momentum

Gain focus, momentum and get as many qualified opportunities in your pipeline as possible.

You have removed any time thieves in your way, you have a created a call list and you have dedicated time to do the one thing that will make you money, which is calling your prospects. Next step you need to take is to build focus and momentum so that you can get as many qualified opportunities in your pipeline as possible.

Holding focused call out days are the best way to achieve this!

During Focus Days you focus on a target, you focus on selling a particular product or service and you focus on getting as many sales opportunities in your pipeline as possible. Focus days work great in sales teams where days can sometimes feel quite monotonous and you can easily fall into a routine. Focus days break the routine and get you away from day-to-day norm and in doing so they help you create a buzz in the office on the day and accelerate your performance.

Focus days work best when you have a team of sales people working with you so, if you are part of a team take responsibility for organising the call out day and convince your team to take part. You will have great fun as team when you run a focus day and more importantly, you will all achieve increased sales results.

To organise a focus day you will need to do the following:

- Decide on a particular product or service that you would like to sell more of. Choose one that you do have in stock and that you can complete a sale in within the next six weeks.
- Review the chosen product or service with your team members and look at the pain it reduces or removes and the gain it provides prospects with, then select a target prospect market that has the most need for your product or service.
- Ensure all sales people have the chosen prospect data available before starting the focus day so that you can maximise call times and limit the amount of time spent looking for data in your internal systems. I have always used a simple Excel sheet to hold the prospects data and it has always worked extremely well as you can simply print it out and call one prospect after the other.
- Identify any external influences that may affect prospects and encourage them to buy.
- Create a prospect incentive that will encourage them to take action today.
- Plan your prime selling time and ensure that everybody agrees to stick to it! I would even recommend that you ask the team to shut their email system down until the agreed admin times.
- Next, set a target for what you would like to achieve from the focus day. Depending on the product/service and the sales cycle this could be a revenue target (if you can get sales on the day) or it could be a sales opportunity target so that you can build your pipeline with qualified opportunities than you can close in the next six weeks. They key is to set some sort of target so that you can measure success.

How to Treble Your Sales Results in Six Weeks!

- Agree on the best opening statement that you can all use to grab your prospects attention before starting the focus day.
- Identify questions that will identify the pain or gain.
- Agree on how you can create urgency with prospects to gain some form or commitment on the day.
- Break the target for the day down into small achievable chunks and align it to your prime selling time so that you can see that you are on the right track by the end of each of the prime selling times in the day.
- Create a reward and recognition programme to recognise the first opportunities to come in, all sales or opportunities raised, the most effort, the highest opportunity value, number of calls or prospect visits etc. Giving CD's, DVD's, vouchers and alcohol always work as great prizes for call out days so I highly recommend that you invest in some of these prizes before the call out day so that you have the physical prizes to reward great performance on the day.
- Create a tracker board where team members physically have to write up the name of the opportunity they have won. This is a really important pat of the focus day as it creates excitement, gets the competitive spirit going and increases motivation to get back on the phones or visit more prospects as it feels great to go up and put your achievement on the board.
- Make the focus day fun and exciting.
- Celebrate your success at the end of the day!

To treble your sales results in six weeks I would suggest that you start your campaign to treble your sales results by holding a focus day so that you build the excitement, momentum and your sales pipeline. You will see the success that you can achieve by focusing and the benefit of holding them after your first one so make a plan to hold at least one a week for the next six weeks so that you are continuously building focus and your pipeline!

Chapter 7: Building & Sustaining Individual Motivation

If you were a small business would you run your business without having a watertight business plan?

If you ran a blue chip company would you run the company without having a vision of where you are going, agreed goals that you need to achieve and a strategy in place to help you achieve your goals?

Well you could, however, you would not be very successful!

If you fail to plan, you plan to fail.

As a sales person, you are running your own business because you run your own territory or have a set of prospects to develop. However, many sales people I have met over the years still do not have their own business plan or goals in place to ensure that they are successful.

It is not enough to wait for your sales mangers to give you your targets and have a one-to-one to discuss your priorities. To be successful in sales and to treble your own sales results in six weeks you will need your own business plan and targets. By having a clear plan of where you are going, you will hugely increase your level of motivation and confidence and your chances of your reaching your desired goals.

To help you create your business plan, here is a step by step process which you can follow to ensure you reach your final destination – which in this case will be to treble your sales results in six weeks!

Set Your Six Week Target

Step 1 – Set powerful goals.

The first step to successfully creating a business plan or action plan that will enable you to treble your sales results to is to start with the end in mind, so that means setting your target for what you are going to achieve when you treble your sales results!

> *"Start with the end in mind"*
> Stephen Covey

When a business sets a growth target they generally set a target to beat last years results so that they can have a like for like comparison. In this case we are going to use a six week period as our like for like comparison therefore to set your target, simply look at your average sales achievement in the six week period prior to reading this book and then treble it!!! Whatever figure you have reached, you now need to make that your goal and make it happen.

Before turning your figure into a powerful goal that you will achieve I would like to help you understand the difference between a true powerful goal and a 'wish list'.

Goals enable us to achieve excellence. They are specific, they are targeted and they get us to the end point in our journey. They give us more focus; more purpose, more direction and more motivation.

A 'wish list' is unspecific, unfocused, not targeted and does not offer you more focus and motivation as it is simply a dream or a nice to have.

I meet so many sales people who really want to treble their sales results however some of them are dreamers and others are achievers. Dreamers have trebling their sales results in their wish list, they live on what I call 'some day I'll...'. The achievers set really powerful goals and take positive action everyday to achieve their goals. To stop being a dreamer and become a true achiever take trebling sales results off your wish list and turn it into a powerful goal that you are totally committed to.

A powerful goal is always written down and should be written using some proven goal setting rules. They should be:

- **Positive** – What you want not what you don't want.
- **Personal** – I am, I have, I am doing.
- **Present Tense** - you have achieved them.

Powerful goals are:

- Specific.
- Inspiring.
- Measureable.
- Time bound.
- Congruent with values.
- Within your control to achieve.
- Written down.
- Referred to regularly and updated .
- Actions set for each that will help you to achieve them.

As an example a wish list or dreamers' goals would be written as:

I will try to treble my sales results.

Achievers' goals would be written as:

I have trebled my sales results in six weeks.

By writing your goals, using the goal setting rules, you are writing them as if you have already achieved them and this in itself will help you to focus on a daily basis to ensure that you achieve it.

So now set yourself a goal for the next six weeks using the goal setting rules.

```
My Goal:



```

Congratulations, you now have a clear goal in place! Your next step is to achieve it!

> *"Setting goals is one thing however*
> *achieving them is another'"*
> Stephen Covey

To actually achieve your goal there are three things you need:

- Motivation.
- A clear action plan.
- Commitment.

Set Your Personal & Sales Goals

Step 2 - Building individual motivation.

Without personal motivation, you are highly unlikely to succeed in trebling your sales results in six weeks. I can teach you everything that you need to do to achieve your goal of trebling your sales results however, without motivation, you simply won't take action which is why motivation is one the key contributors to achieving this goal. If you look up the word motivation in the dictionary you will find that the meaning of the word is:

Building & Sustaining Individual Motivation

- **Motivate – to cause or stimulate a person to act, the underlying cause.**

In the world of sales, I see motivation as:
- A state or readiness or eagerness.
- An internal state that is influenced by external factors.
- About the action we take – including the action of doing nothing!
- A state, which cannot be imposed, but is discovered, built and sustained from within by each individual.

Every sales person is motivated, however few know how to identify and sustain their personal motivation.

Some think that sales people are motivated by hitting targets. I strongly disagree as hitting targets is not what really drives their motivation. What really drives their motivation is <u>what they get as a result</u> of hitting their targets.

I was talking at a sales seminar for sales leaders and managers who had come from all over the world. To start the seminar I asked all of the sales leaders to put up their hands if they felt that hitting target was a valid goal and of course everyone put their hand up.

Once they had their hands raised I told them they were all wrong as a target is not a sales person's goal and in fact, any sales person that tells you hitting targets is their goal is probably a very demotivated individual. All of the hands went down.

I had created a state of confusion, which they did not understand or like however; it was my intention to do this. You see a sales target is not a sales person's goal; it is merely a means to achieving their own personal goals. Then I asked them to write down the answers to the following questions:

- What is your main reason for waking up and coming to work each day?
- What goal are you trying to achieve?

- What motivates you to take the actions that will help you to achieve your goals?

What do you think their answers were? Do you think they all said they come to work to hit targets or did they come to work because they wanted to achieve something personally?

Of course they wanted to achieve something personally. People only take action when they are motivated to do so and when it takes them in a direction that is positive for them. They don't come to work just to keep the boss happy by hitting target. Now they were starting to understand the method behind my madness.

As sales people, we know that our prospects are only motivated to buy when they can see the value add or the 'what's in it for them' and sales people are the same. If we cannot see what's in it for us we don't take action!

When we can see the real 'what's in it for us', then we are motivated to take action. So, bearing this in mind, if we know that we are motivated by what we gain as a result of achieving targets and if we keep that in the forefront of our minds, we will build and sustain our own individual and inner motivation which in turn will increase our chances of trebling our sales results.

So what is the real motivation for you? What's in it for you to take action everyday to achieve your target of trebling your sales results?

I remember when I got my first a 'real' sales job with Yellow Pages. Targets were huge and there was no room for underperformance!

It was three strikes or you are out so I knew that from the start I had to ensure that I was motivated to achieve! To build and sustain my motivation I set myself a personal goal to move from a house I was renting in Surbiton to buying a house of my own. Every day I reminded myself that I was going to work to buy my house, I dreamed about what it would look like and what I would feel like when I finally moved in. On the days when things got tough I simply reminded myself of that feeling to get myself into the right state of mind to continue taking positive action and it worked every time. I associated coming to work and hitting target as a means to achieve my personal goals.

Within one year, I achieved my goal. I raised £40 000 as a deposit for my new house and I bought a lovely three bedroom house which was the ultimate dream for me as the house I had been renting was tiny and only had one bedroom.

The house motivated me to take action and I knew that if I made more phone calls, talked to the right prospects, signed more new business, over-achieved targets and earned more commission every month, I would get the deposit for my house.

I sustained my motivation by reminding myself how good it would feel when I finally achieved it and this put me into a positive frame of mind and really helped to achieved better sales figures.

Build And Sustain Individual Motivation

What does trebling your sales results mean to you?

To build your motivation so that you can treble your sales results in the next six weeks, I would highly recommend that you set yourself a personal goal that you can remind yourself of on a daily basis to sustain your motivation and achieve your goals.

Your personal goal could be like mine which was to buy a new house. It could be to buy a new car, be put forward for promotion, because you want to gain some recognition or it could be that you want to be the top performer in your team. Whatever your goal is, you must write it down using the goal setting rules that we looked at in the previous chapters.

How to Treble Your Sales Results in Six Weeks!

I would like you to take yourself forward by six weeks, visualise yourself having achieved your goal. See what you see, hear what you hear and feel what you feel.

What you are saying to yourself, feeling or hearing?

In the box below, I would like you to describe your personal goal and what it is like when you achieve it.

My Personal Goal is:

What are you saying to yourself, feeling, or hearing?

To sustain your individual motivation you can remind yourself of this on a daily basis. By doing so, you will really build your momentum and motivation and it helps you to understand that every time you take positive action *now*, you are getting one step closer to achieving your personal goal!!!

Identify Your Key Priorities

Step 3 - Identify your key priorities.

Now that you have a clear personal goal and can see how trebling your sales results will benefit you can start to create a detailed action plan for success.

Building & Sustaining Individual Motivation

The first step to creating a detailed action plan is to identify the key priorities that you need to focus on in order to achieve your goal. The priorities you select should all take you one-step close to achieving your personal goal.
Please list up to six areas that you feel should be a priority for you to focus on.

1:

2:

3:

4:

5:

6:

Example - Priorities that you may need to focus on:

- Your attitude – believe and achieve.
- Implement all of your new sales techniques.
- Gain focus and momentum to build your pipeline .
- Implement a prime selling time.
- Create a prospect penetration matrix.
- Sustain personal motivation.
- Win more new business.
- Monitor and measure your success.

Step 4 – Setting a final goal for each key priority.

Next you need to establish a final goal for each of the priority areas. By breaking the big goal, which is to treble your sales results in six weeks into smaller achievable chunks (your key priorities) you will make what may have appeared as impossible into something that is possible if you simply take it step by step.

Please set a final goal using the goals setting rules for each of your key priorities. As an example, productivity should be one of your key priorities and the final goal should be 'I have achieved three hours talk time by the end of July'.

Final Goals:

1:

2:

3:

4:

5:

6:

Step 4– Identifying your current strengths.

The next step is to identify what you are already doing well that you would like to keep and to identify any strengths that you use in other areas of your life that will enable you achieve your goal of trebling your sales results.

In my public seminars I run a similar exercise to help sales people recognise their strengths and believe it or not, this is the exercise they find most difficult. So many sales people can tell me what they **are not** good at and they really struggle to identify what they are good at. This doesn't mean that they are not good at anything it simply means that they are focusing on what they are not good at more than their strengths. To identify your strength in each of your key priorities look at:

⇨ What positive things are going on in that area?

⇨ What's working well?

⇨ What skills have you got?

⇨ What helpful habits do you already have?

Some of the strengths you have may overlap into all of the priorities you have. This is great as it means you can utilise each of your skills in multiple areas of your work.

If you are finding identifying your strengths difficult then you could:

- Ask your colleagues, your friends and your customers what they feel you are good at and remind yourself of these strengths on a daily basis to instil more belief in yourself.
- Think back to the exercise we did in chapter one when I told you I was going to give you a Ferrari for £50k but you could sell it for £150k, what did you do and what strength did you use or find in yourself that ensured you made the £100k profit.

Remove Barriers to Your Success

We all have so many strengths yet it can sometimes feel more natural to identify what you need to improve on. Once you have identified your strengths, talk about them on a more regular basis and then this will feel more natural to you and best of all, you actually start to believe them, which can really build both your confidence and motivation.

How to Treble Your Sales Results in Six Weeks!

Step 5 –Identify barriers to success.

Have you ever set yourself a goal and failed? Most people have and the failure is due to a lack of commitment or, they faced a barrier on the way that either threw them off their path or made it appear more difficult to achieve.

To achieve any goals there is always an element of change involved and when change is involved, there will be more often than not, barriers that you will need to face.

People, who set goals and fail, do so because they did not plan how they could overcome their barriers at the start. Instead, when the barrier hit them along the way they fell at the first hurdle or stopped trying.

If you are to achieve your goal of trebling your sales results, you should firstly identify any barriers that you think YOU may face at the start so that, as part of your action plan, you can identify the actions you need to take in order to overcome them.

Performance = Potential – Interference
Tim Galloway 'The Inner game of Tennis'

To identify any barriers that you feel you may face, answer these questions:

- What might stop you moving forward?
- What might get in your way?
- What barriers will you have to overcome?
- Is this really a barrier or an excuse?

If the barrier is real, ask yourself:

- How can you overcome this barrier?
- Who can help you to overcome this barrier?
- How have you successfully negotiated this barrier previously?

- What strengths have you already got that will help you to overcome this barrier?
- Is the barrier within your control?
- What resources could you use to overcome this barrier?

By simply creating a plan to overcome barriers in advance you will reduce or completely remove any barriers that could have limited in your success in achieving your goal.

Step 6 – *"Goals without actions are just a way of filling your day"* – Tony Robbins

How do you eat an elephant?'

The answer of course, is one slice at a time!

To achieve all of your final goals it is advisable to break them down into smaller chunks or smaller actions. By achieving all of the smaller actions, a slice at a time, you will eventually get to eat the elephant and treble your sales results!

Achieving agreed actions is a great marker for you as it helps you to check that you are on the right track and doing all of the right things to achieving your goals.

Therefore, using the goal setting rules, create a set of actions for each of your key priorities and final goals. The actions, when completed should take you towards achieving your final goal. When setting your actions remind yourself of all the strengths that you already have which will enable you to achieve your goal.

As an example a final goal could be:

'I have achieved £300k in sales which has trebled my sales results in six weeks'

So the smaller actions would be:

- I have achieved £50k in sales results by week one.

How to Treble Your Sales Results in Six Weeks!

- I have achieved £100k in sales results by week two.
- I have achieved £150k in sales results by week three.
- I have achieved £200k in sales results by week four.
- I have achieved £250k in sales results by week five.
- I have achieved £300k in sales results by week six.

By taking all of these actions you reach your final destination and achieve your goal of trebling your sales results!!!!

Create Your Action Plan For Success

Create a set of actions that will enable you to achieve your final goals in each of the key priorities:

Week 1

Week 2

Week 3

Week 4

Week 5

Week 6

Commitment

Finally, it is taking positive action everyday that will enable you to achieve your goal of trebling your sales results!

Like Stephen Covey said *"It is one thing to set goals and actions however it is quite another to achieve them."* To achieve them you need motivation and a solid action plan and finally you need commitment!

People who achieve goals all have a high level of commitment. They do not procrastinate over taking action and they don't stop trying because they have a bad day or they are tired, they keep going until they reach their goal.

On a scale of 1 to 10, with 10 being totally committed and 0 being no commitment, achievers and top performers are at a 10. Where is your level of commitment on a scale of 1 -10?

How to Treble Your Sales Results in Six Weeks!

If your level of commitment is under a 10 then I would urge you to go back to your personal goals and ask yourself how much you really want it and how much it means to you. If you really want it then you have to take accountability for achieving it and ownership to making it happen.

Accountability & Ownership

Great achievers take responsibility for their success. They don't rely on managers, the do not rely on quick wins and they don't play the blame game! Great achievers take fully responsibility for their own success, when they succeed they reward themselves and if they fail, then they take responsibility for it and try again and again until they achieve it.

If you consider yourself an achiever rather than a dreamer, remember that achieving the personal goal that you set in the previous chapter is completely within your control when you have a solid plan in place and are committed to tak-i   n   g positive action everyday to achieve it!!!

Make it Happen

Take action and make it happen!

"No one else can sing your song, write your story or dance your dance; you are the designer of your own destiny!"
Buddah

A Closing Message From Fiona

You were probably attracted to this book because the title appealed to you.

When you started reading, you may have questioned if it is really possible to treble your sales results in six weeks and if you can do it. Well it IS possible and other sales people have already more than trebled their sales results as a result of using the techniques that I have introduced to in this book.

So that leaves us with 'can you do it?', and the answer to that is **yes you can!**

You have developed your 'skill factor' by learning all of the new techniques and you have developed your 'will factor' by developing that little thing that makes a big difference…your attitude, and the exciting thing about that is you own it and you control it.

Don't procrastinate and don't make the mistake of falling back into old routines and habits. Instead make the change and take action. When you do, trebling your sales results will be just six weeks away! Only you can make it happen!

"The definition of Madness is doing the same thing in the same way, over and over again and expecting a different result"
Tony Robbins

I wish you good luck in your journey to achieving both your sales and personal goals. Enjoy the journey and please do let me know about the amazing results you achieve!

Good Luck!

Fiona

The Next Step

'Explode Your Sales Results And Boost Your Profits by joining me at my Next 'Live Strategic Selling Workshop'

Top performers like famous sports professionals are action-orientated people who are committed to taking the right actions as they immediately implement strategies and ideas that they learn from books or training sessions.

They do not hesitate and they do not procrastinate! However, through experience, I know that even the best sales people with the greatest intentions of implementing the strategies and ideas you have learnt in this book can unintentionally fail. Why does this happen?

In sales, it is so easy to fall back into your normal routine. You read books like this at lunchtime or in the evening however, when you return to your normal workday, there may be prospects who are waiting for a call back. You may have appointments you need to attend and quotes that need to be issued. Your inbox may be full of emails from prospects, your forecast may need to be updated. For some, the pressure may be on to hit target. The list goes on and on and before you know it, you are back into your old routine and the ideas and strategies that you have learnt remain as simply ideas.

To turn ideas into action, to achieve your goal of trebling your sales results you need to dedicate time to creating a strategy. This means taking time out of your daily activities and disruptions so that you can work on your business rather than in it.

To perfect your skills you need practice implementing all of them until you find a formula that works specifically for you and your business.

To increase your 'will factor' you need to work on changing your behaviour, increase your belief, your confidence and your motivation. Doing all of this by yourself in a busy sales environment where you are under pressure to hit targets is never easy, which is why I have created our three-day intensive 'Strategic Selling Workshop'.

This 3 day intensive strategic selling workshop is the ultimate solution for any sales person, sales leader or business owner wanting to treble their sales results, control their targets instead of letting targets control them and gain it in the fastest possible way with less stress and with the help of leading experts! Attending the strategic selling workshop allows you take some time out with an expert team.

At our strategic selling workshop you will turn ideas into action and create a sales strategy that will ensure you become a high performing sales person. You will acquire all of the skills, tools and techniques to become confident in selling, you will gain help from experts to change your behaviour and your results.

We achieve all of this is a friendly and comfortable environment with like minded professionals and with no distractions of the phone ringing or a prospect trying to get hold of you. However make no mistake; this is not a garden party!

At the workshop, we work long hours and we work extremely hard to ensure that in three days you perfect a sales strategy and hone your skills so that, you are ready to implement every idea and strategy immediately upon your return to work.

After attending the workshop you will also receive mentoring sessions with Fiona Challis to sustain your motivation and ensure you take the right actions. In your sessions you can also bounce ideas off or, discuss any challenges you are facing with Fiona so that we get things moving in the right direction for you in the fastest possible time.

At the workshop you will learn thousands of pounds worth of additional sales strategies and ideas from Fiona and other leading sales experts.

You will leave with increased confidence and motivation,

a watertight plan to achieve your desired results, a 75 page workbook and a choice of a CD or DVD recording of the entire three days so that you can refresh your skills at any time.

You will also have a one to one consultation with Fiona during the three days, to create a bespoke sales strategy to maximise your business potential and then accept a series of follow up mentoring calls to help you implement everything you have learnt as you treble you sales results within six weeks!

At the workshop, we only want people who are willing to work hard and willing to take action because everyone attending will be held accountable for trebling their sales results in six weeks. To be accepted on the workshop you must meet some qualifying criteria:

You must:

- Really want to treble your sales results.
- Be action orientated.
- Be willing to learn from others.
- Be willing to work hard.
- Be willing to try new ideas.
- Be willing to share your sales challenges with others.
- Have methods to monitor or measure your success or be willing to take advice on how you can achieve this.
- Be willing to start implementing the sales strategy we help you to create immediately.

If you really want to treble your sales results and you meet all of the above qualifying criteria then please:

Visit www.salesconversionexpert.com to view available dates.

Or call 01189 767658 if you have any questions you would like us to answer.

I look forward to meeting you at theworkshop.

Good Luck

Fiona

What Others Say About Working With Fiona

What clients say about working with Fiona and how implementing her ideas and strategies have benefited their businesses......

"Working with Fiona has transformed the potential of my business into reality. The passion I have for my business was matched by Fiona and she provided me with wise counsel and a priceless insight into the world of what my clients actually want. After making a few adjustments to my proposition and marketing methods, sales rocketed and business boomed...this girl is good...No, she is great!"

Scott Hodson, OF Software

'Dear Fiona, I want to thank you for the amazing sales strategy you gave me. My product is a high price item and so needs to be explained in a manner that will remove price objections. Your strategy to remove the 'fear barrier' and move them to seeing they cannot do without it is simply brilliant. I decided to use the strategy immediately and have since converted four clients, two of whom I had already spoken with and who were 'not sure'. That's £8000 worth of new business in just two weeks! Thank you'

Don Hastie

"Fiona's amazing enthusiasm and flair for her subject is infectious and she is able to share her knowledge in way that makes sense. I have applied everything that she has taught me to my business, re-trained my team, tweaked our messages and fundamentally revamped our marketing. With just one technique I increased my database by over 200 leads in 24 hours and have so far converted 30 of those leads which equates to £30,000 increase in turnover per year, every year. More will follow. Not bad for just one technique!"

Wendy Shand, Founder of Tots to Travel

"Our management team were beginning to believe increasing volume sales would be impossible; the approach Fiona used increased sales results by over 400%. The sales campaign was a tremendous success and the processes and principals implemented by Fiona are now the departmental standard in selling our general product and service portfolio to the SME market"

Evan Garricks (GM, Head of Sales – MTN Business)

"I wouldn't hesitate recommending Fiona to any of my clients. She over delivered in passion and enthusiasm for the training"

Senior Sales Manager, Canadean

"I would recommend Fiona to any business that need to find ways to re-engage their sales forces"

Senior Sales Director

"This is by far one the most structured and useful training sessions that I have attended to date"

Sales Manager, Zebra Technologies

"The knowledge transfer in this course is extremely valuable as it provides a proven methodology for raising the level of performance of both individuals and teams"

Sales Manager, BMC Software

"A superb course that provides the skills, motivation and attitude to get my sales team to excel. Highly recommended!"

Andy Cleet, Imago

"Highly recommended, extremely useful to any business which is struggling to find ways of empowering their sales managers and proactively engaging their sales people"

Sales Manager, Scheuco

"Fiona really addressed some key issues we are facing within our team. We are now far better equipped to deal with them"

Sales Manager, Integralis

"Fiona is a truly outstanding leader. Her energy, execution capability, creativity and self motivation are outstanding. Results are team oriented and it is really easy to work with her. I especially applaud her ability to work under tight deadlines. Definitely a manager I'd have in my own team"

Javier Perea, McAfee International

"Fiona delivered professional and structured training sessions with an acute sensitivity for the team members' need as well as for the company's and its clients' needs. Her enthusiasm, friendliness and radiant personality are a recipe for success"

GB, Partners in Europe

"Fiona is an exceptional sales leader with a strong understanding of how to grow business, and motivate people. Fiona's business acumen, market knowledge and sales experience proved invaluable in driving sustained growth and success. An asset to any company she is associated with"

Sean Glynn

"I would recommend this course to ant sales person wishing to move themselves to the next level"

Account Manager, Auto Trader

"Really enjoyed the course. Learned lots about sales techniques and myself. Fiona is extremely approachable and helped me to remove my negative views and build on my confidence"

Sales Representative, Aston Lloyd

"The level of energy and enthusiasm definitely inspired me to look at my own attitudes and how I can become more motivated"

Account Manager, FEXCO

"I would recommend this trainer to anyone, very concise, clear and full of enthusiasm"

Sales Representative, Trader media

"I have learn so much in sales and building rapport with prospects. Fiona instils belief, passion, drive and has provided me al of the tool I need"

Sales Representative

"I felt that my skills have improved greatly. Also had the chance to analyse myself and discover how to move forward"

P. Lamb Forrester

"Fiona helped me to see that people can achieve anything as a results of motivation and asking the right questions"

Ayo, MTN

"The skills provided give you the ability to earn whatever you wish"

Alphesh

"I has so many 'light bulb' moments and cant wait to put them into practice" –

Jo Jo, Forever Living

"Uplifting and Positive"

Heather, Warners